PEANUTS
The loves of Snoopy

by
SCHULZ

HODDER AND STOUGHTON
LONDON SYDNEY AUCKLAND TORONTO

ISBN 0 340 22755 9 (cased edition)
ISBN 0 340 24581 6 (paperbound edition)

Copyright © 1967, 1968, 1969, 1970, 1971, 1972, 1973
by United Feature Syndicate Inc.

First published 1978 (cased)

First published 1979 (paperbound)

Printed in Belgium for Hodder and Stoughton Children's Books
a division of Hodder & Stoughton Ltd,
Mill Road, Dunton Green, Sevenoaks, Kent
(Editorial Office: 47 Bedford Square, London, WC1B 3DP)
by Henri Proost & Cie, Turnhout

IS LOVE A 'NOW' KIND OF THING, CHUCK, OR IS IT MOSTLY HOPE AND MEMORIES?

WELL, MY DAD SAYS THAT HE TOOK A GIRL TO THE MOVIES ONCE, AND IT WAS ONE OF THOSE REAL SAD LOVE STORIES...

HE REMEMBERED THAT ANNE BAXTER WAS IN IT, AND FOR YEARS AFTERWARD, EVERY TIME HE SAW ANNE BAXTER, HE'D GET REAL DEPRESSED BECAUSE IT WOULD REMIND HIM OF THAT MOVIE AND THE GIRL HE HAD BEEN WITH...

HE NEVER FORGOT THAT GIRL BECAUSE EVERY TIME HE SAW ANNE BAXTER, IT WOULD REMIND HIM OF HER...

THEN, ONE NIGHT ON THE LATE, SHOW, THAT SAME MOVIE CAME ON, BUT IT TURNED OUT THAT HE HAD BEEN WRONG ALL THOSE YEARS... IT WASN'T ANNE BAXTER... IT WAS SUSAN HAYWARD!

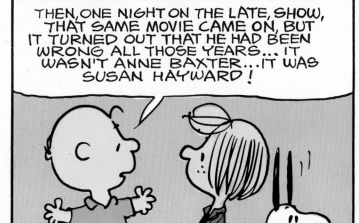

LOVE HAS ITS MEMORIES I GUESS.

I WAS REALLY HOPING IT WAS A 'NOW' KIND OF THING.

IT IS FOR SOME OF US, SWEETIE!

I'VE NEVER SEEN IT TO FAIL!

FIND A GOOD SPOT AND EVERYONE ELSE MOVES IN!

QUESTION...

WHAT DO YOU THINK THE SECRET OF LOVING IS, CHUCK?

THE SECRET OF LIVING IS TO OWN A CONVERTIBLE AND A LAKE...

A CONVERTIBLE AND A LAKE?

IF THE SUN IS SHINING, YOU CAN RIDE AROUND IN YOUR CONVERTIBLE AND BE HAPPY... IF IT STARTS TO RAIN, IT WON'T SPOIL YOUR DAY BECAUSE YOU CAN JUST SAY, "OH, WELL, THE RAIN WILL FILL UP MY LAKE!"

WHAT DO YOU THINK THE SECRET OF LIVING IS, SNOOPY?

SMAK!

A CONVERTIBLE AND A LAKE... I DON'T KNOW ABOUT YOU, CHUCK...

IF YOUR LAKE IS DRYING UP, YOU CAN SAY, "OH WELL, THIS IS NICE WEATHER FOR RIDING IN A CONVERTIBLE..!"

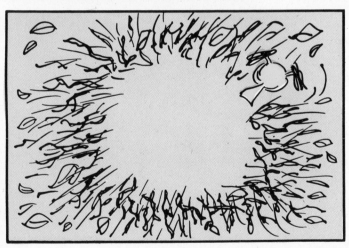

9

THINGS LIKE THAT COULD RUIN SPECTATOR SPORTS...

HE'S COMING! HE'S COMING!

THANK YOU, EASTER BEAGLE! THANK YOU!

THANK YOU!

THANK YOU VERY MUCH...

THANK YOU

THANK YOU!

EVERYBODY GETS AN EGG FROM THE EASTER BEAGLE!

WHO DO I GET ONE FROM?

HIS ASSISTANT!

Their love was not
in the Cards

"You've always ignored me"
she said. "And now you say
you want to marry me."

"Every night you play cards."

"I'm really afraid," she said,
"that you love cards more
than you love me."

"If you could say something
nice to me just once, perhaps
I'd marry you."

" ◇ ♣ ♥ ♠ "

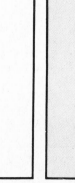

"You blew it!" she said, and
walked out of his life forever.

SCHULZ

HERE YOU GO, OL' PAL...

ENJOY YOUR SUPPER

!

HOLD IT!

I THINK I LEFT SOMETHING OUT...

I'M THE ONLY ONE I KNOW WHO HAS EVER HAD HIS SUPPER RECALLED!

SCHULZ

Dear Contributor,
We regret to inform you that your manuscript does not suit our present needs.

The Editors

P.S. Don't take it out on your mailbox.

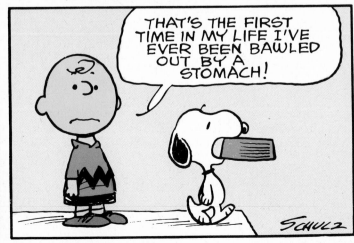

I FORGOT THAT I PROMISED TO TAKE THEM ON A PICNIC TODAY...

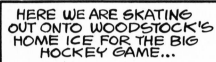
HERE WE ARE SKATING OUT ONTO WOODSTOCK'S HOME ICE FOR THE BIG HOCKEY GAME...

AND HERE COME THE OFFICIALS...

THE REFEREE

THE LINESMEN

THE GOAL JUDGES AND THE PENALTY TIMEKEEPER

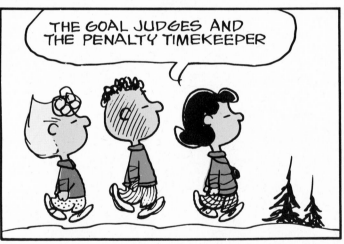

THE OFFICIAL SCORER AND THE GAME TIMEKEEPER!

WHICH BRINGS UP A SLIGHT PROBLEM...

WHERE DO WE PUT THE ORGAN FOR THE NATIONAL ANTHEM?

SCHULZ

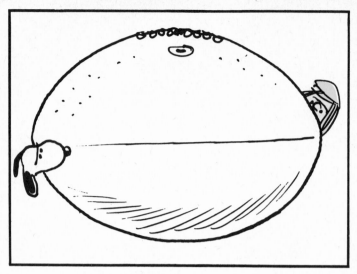

NOPE!

I'D LIKE TO HAVE YOU ON MY TEAM, CHUCK, BUT I JUST DON'T THINK YOU'RE GOOD ENOUGH...

IN FACT I DON'T SEE ANYONE AROUND HERE WHO COULD COME UP TO MY STANDARD!

HOW ABOUT MY LINEBACKER OVER THERE? HE'S PRETTY GOOD

HIM?

OKAY, LET'S TRY HIM OUT...

HERE I COME, FELLA! STOP ME IF YOU CAN!!

FREIGHT TRAIN!!

CRUNCH! RIB-SHAKING FLESH-TEARING TEETH RATTLING

BONE-BREAKING EAR-SPLITTING EARTH SHATTERING

SMASH!

GOOD SHOT, KID! HOW WOULD YOU LIKE TO PLAY FOR A DECENT TEAM?

SIGH

KEEP TALKING SWEETIE...

33

WELL, PERHAPS I CAN CLEAR UP A LITTLE MISCONCEPTION FOR YOU

SNOWSTORMS ARE NOT CAUSED BY KICKING A SNOWMAN!

WHEW

SIGH

I TOLD THEM THAT I THOUGHT THEY WERE TOO YOUNG, AND THAT RUNNING AWAY NEVER SOLVES ANYTHING...

I THINK THEY'LL BOTH BE GLAD THAT HE CAME TO ME FOR ADVICE...

BOOT!

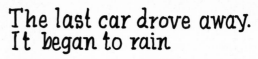The last car drove away.
It began to rain

And so our hero's life
ended as it had begun...
a disaster.

"I never got any breaks,"
he had always complained.

He had wanted to be rich.
He died poor. He wanted
friends. He died friendless.

He wanted to be loved. He
died unloved. He wanted
laughter. He found only tears

He wanted applause. He received
boos. He wanted fame. He found
only obscurity. He wanted
answers. He found only questions.

I'M HAVING
A HARD
TIME ENDING
THIS...

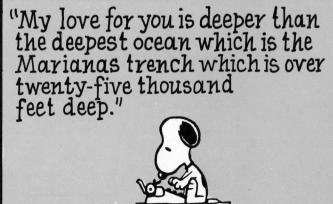

40

43

HE'S NOT VERY FRIENDLY, IS HE?

YOU COULD SAY THAT

WHAT DO YOU THINK WOULD HAPPEN IF I TURNED AROUND AND GAVE HIM A BIG KISS?

WHO KNOWS?

HOW SHOULD I DO IT? JUST WHIRL AROUND, AND KISS HIM?

WHY NOT?

SMAK

BLEAHH!!

"BLEAHH"?!

YOU MUSICIANS ARE SOMETHING ELSE!

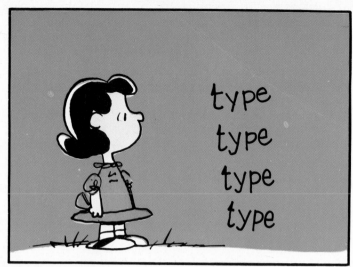

type
type
type
type

Toodle-oo Caribou!
A Tale of the
Frozen North

The stall was empty
"Someone has stolen my
polar cow" shouted
Joe Eskimo

"This is the work
of Joe Jacket
who hates me!"

MAY I SEE HOW YOUR NEW NOVEL IS COMING ALONG?

BE MY GUEST

"JOE ESKIMO AND JOE JACKET WERE RIVALS FOR THE HEART OF SALLY SNOW WHO LIVED SOUTH OF THE ICEBERG... JOE ESKIMO THOUGHT BACK TO THE NIGHT HE FIRST SHOOK HER HAND"

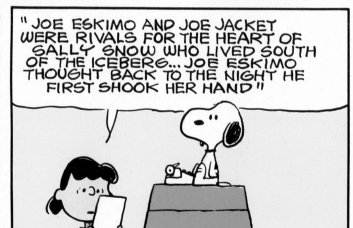

"I THINK YOU ARE VERY NICE" HE HAD TOLD HER, AND THEY SHOOK HANDS.

THEY SHOOK HANDS?

I THINK YOUR LOVE SCENE NEEDS A LITTLE SOMETHING...

I ALWAYS GET SO EMBARRASSED

45